From the Curse of Willie Lynch to the Awakening

By JAMES C. ROLLINS

Order this book online at www.trafford.com
or email orders@trafford.com

Most Trafford titles are also available at major online book retailers.

Note for Librarians: A cataloguing record for this book is available from Library
and Archives Canada at www.collectionscanada.ca/amicus/index-e.html

Printed in Victoria, BC, Canada.

ISBN: 978-1-4269-1802-5 (sc)
ISBN: 978-1-4269-2010-3 (hc)

*Our mission is to efficiently provide the world's finest, most comprehensive book publishing
service, enabling every author to experience success. To find out how to publish your book, your
way, and have it available worldwide, visit us online at www.trafford.com*

Trafford rev. 12/22/09

www.trafford.com

North America & international
toll-free: 1 888 232 4444 (USA & Canada)
phone: 250 383 6864 ♦ fax: 812 355 4082

Acknowledgments

WITHOUT THE LOVE AND encouragement of family and friends, this book and the previous one (The Curse of Willie Lynch) would not have been written. This journey started with a question to me from my youngest about her ability to compete in society. Ultimately she not only proved that she could compete, she competed with honors. I will be forever grateful to her for the stimulation to accomplish this endeavor. Thanks Margo.

Traci, my elder daughter blessed me with the new love of my life a granddaughter, Autumn Kennidy and Monee

Sean, my baby boy, has always been a quiet, yet strong influence on my life. Marcia, his daughter- my granddaughter has always been my Miss Sunshine.

Darryl, my elder son gifted me with three super special granddaughters, Kimberly, Brandy, and Shari. Kimberly blessed me with Jalyn making me a great granddad.

Most people go through life having only one or two real friends. I have been blessed with several Edward G. Smith, and   R. Edward Kennedy, friends for forty years and Miji Bell, and Jeanette Mayo all provided much needed editing, encouragement and support. They also provided encouragement when my spirit needed it.

Finally, Francis, Ann, Paul, Yolanda, and Ronauld my forever supportive and encouraging sisters and brothers.

Contents

Introduction ... ix

1. Schools of Dreams ... 1
2. School to Career ... 16
3. Black Wealth ... 23
4. The New Politics in America ... 34
5. Next Generation ... 38
6. The Power of My Money ... 42
7. It Takes A Village ... 44
8. Media Matter ... 48
9. Summary ... 51
   Foot Notes ... 55

"I just want to do God's will. And He's allowed me to go up to the mountain. And I've looked over. And I've seen the Promised Land. I may not get there with you. But I want you to know tonight, that we, as a people will get to the Promised Land."

Martin Luther King
April 3, 1968, Memphis, Tenn.

INTRODUCTION

FORTY YEARS OF WANDERING IN THE WILDERNESS TO THE PROMISED LAND

FOR FORTY YEARS AFTER the death of Martin Luther King, African Americans wondered in the wilderness of American society. The wondering was the results of the 300 year exodus from slavery. For forty years, as with the Jew's exodus from Egypt, African Americans struggled to find their identity, their moral center, their sense of self worth.

The start of the forty year journey began with the death of Martin Luther King in 1968, and ended with the election of Barack Obama to the presidency in 2008. During that journey, we spent much of the past 40 years trying to deprogram from a slave mentality, planned family destruction, premeditated drug addiction of a race of people, de-education of generations through a grossly inferior education systems, economic destruction through financially predatory programs, and finally an insidious daily bombardment of propaganda designed to destroy any sense of self worth.

The journey began with the following speech given on April 3, 1968 by Martin Luther King to the striking sanitation workers in Memphis, Tenn. the night before a planned march in support of the Memphis sanitation workers. The following is an edited version of the full speech:

"As you know, if I were standing at the beginning of time, with the possibility of general and panoramic view of the whole human history up to now, and the Almighty said to me, "Martin Luther King, which age would you like to live in?"-- I would take my mental flight to Egypt through, or rather across the Red Sea, through the wilderness on toward the Promised Land. Today, whether they are in Johannesburg, South Africa; Nairobi, Kenya: Accra, Ghana; New York City; Atlanta, Georgia; Jackson, Mississippi; or Memphis, Tennessee--the cry is always the same--"We want to be free."

Now, what does all of this mean in this great period of history? It means that we've got to stay together. We've got to stay together and maintain unity. You know, whenever Pharaoh wanted to prolong the period of slavery in Egypt, he had a favorite formula for doing it. What was that? He kept the slaves fighting among themselves. But whenever the slaves get together, something happens in Pharaoh's court, and he cannot hold the slaves in slavery. When the slaves get together, that's the beginning of getting out of slavery. Now let us maintain unity.

Now the other thing we'll have to do is this: Always anchor our external direct action with the power of economic withdrawal. Now, we are poor people, individually, we are poor when you compare us with white society in America. We are poor. Never stop and forget that collectively, that means all of us together, collectively we are richer than all the nations in the world, with the exception of nine. Did you ever think about that? After you leave the United States, Soviet Russia, Great Britain, West Germany, France, and I could name the others, the Negro collectively is richer than most nations of the world. We have an annual income of more than thirty billion dollars a year, which is more than all of the exports of the United States, and more than the national budget of Canada. Did you know that? That's power right there, if we know how to pool it.

We don't have to argue with anybody. We don't have to curse and go around acting bad with our words. We don't need any bricks and bottles, we don't need any Molotov cocktails, we just need to go around to these stores, and to these massive industries in our country, and say, "God sent us by here to say to you that you're not treating his children right. And we've come by here to ask you to make the first item on your agenda--fair treatment, where God's children are concerned. Now, if you are not prepared to do that, we do have an agenda that we must follow. And our agenda calls for withdrawing economic support from you."

And so, as a result of this, we are asking you tonight, to go out and tell your neighbors not to buy Coca-Cola in Memphis. Go by and tell them not to buy Sealtest milk. Tell them not to buy--what is the other bread?--Wonder Bread. And what is the other bread company, Jesse? Tell them not to buy Hart's bread. But not only that, we've got to strengthen black institutions. I call upon you to take your money out of the banks downtown and deposit you money in Tri-State Bank--we want a "bank-in" movement in Memphis. So go by the savings and loan association. I'm not asking you something that we don't do ourselves at SCLC. Judge Hooks and others will tell you that we have an account here in the savings and loan association from the Southern Christian Leadership Conference. We're just telling you to follow what we're doing. Put your money there. You have six or seven black insurance companies in Memphis. Take out your insurance there. We want to have an "insurance-in."

Now there are some practical things we can do. We begin the process of building a greater economic base. And at the same time, we are putting pressure where it really hurts. I ask you to follow through here.

And they were telling me, now it doesn't matter now. It really doesn't matter what happens now. I left Atlanta this morning, and as we got started on the plane, there were six of us, the pilot said over the public address system, "We are sorry for the delay, but we have Dr. Martin Luther King on the plane. And to be sure that all of the bags were checked, and to be sure that nothing would be wrong with the plane, we had to check out everything carefully. And we've had the plane protected and guarded all night."

And then I got into Memphis. And some began to say that threats, or talk about the threats that were out. What would happen to me from some of our sick white brothers?

Well, I don't know what will happen now. We've got some difficult days ahead. But it doesn't matter with me now. Because I've been to the mountain top. And I don't mind. Like anybody, I would like to live a long life. Longevity has its place. But I'm not concerned about that now. I just want to do God's will. And He's allowed me to go up to the mountain. And I've looked over. And I've seen the Promised Land. I may not get there with you. But I want you to know tonight, that we, as a people will get to the Promised Land. And I'm happy, tonight. I'm not worried about anything. I'm not fearing any man. Mine eyes have seen the glory of the coming of the Lord.

Martin Luther King Jr.[1]

The significance of the above speech was that it was a precursor of the long, hard, and at sometimes frustrating journey upon which African Americans were about to embark. African Americans needed to rediscover who they were; what made them special; and recommit themselves to those values that helped them to survive for more than 300 years in America.

In recent years we have become more educated, more prosperous, and more morally focused. The journey is on-going. The road will still be hard and long. With the election of Barack Obama, black folk are starting to believe in themselves. We have began to realize the dream of Dr. King- "that we, as a people will get to the Promised Land."

In my earlier book – The Curse of Willie Lynch- I tried to point out the historical mental conditioning and learned behaviors that were designed to prevent us from ever realizing our true potential as a race. Today, I am encouraged by the new found confidence, intelligence, and goal oriented mindset of the new generation of black kids. It took forty years and if we "don't let nobody turn us round" we will finally get there.

But first: we must educate ourselves; empower ourselves through an appreciation of our true economic worth; understand that we can significantly impact the politics in this country with our vote; and finally build a moral foundation for future generations to insure that they will never have to again endure what earlier generations had to endure.

1

SCHOOLS OF DREAMS
"There is a brilliant child locked inside every student,"1

DURING A RECENT VISIT to a friend's house, I had an opportunity to observe a one year old kid named Josiah with an interesting problem. He was in the kitchen with his parents riding his scooter. After a while he decided to ride in the hallway; however he had a problem, he could not get his scooter over lip of the doorway into the hall. He first tried to ride over the obstruction without success. He than backed up, got a running start- no success.

After several attempts he stopped and just sat there on his scooter. My first instinct was to help him, but I hesitated for a moment instead. As I moved to help him, he got off the scooter, pulled it up to the obstruction, proceeded to lift the front wheel over the obstruction, walked to the rear where he proceeded to push the scooter's rear wheels to the obstruction. Josiah lifted the rear wheels over the obstruction, mounted his scooter, and proceeded happily down the hallway.

I mention this incident because a number of things happened that dispelled the myth that black kids are inferior. I don't think that Josiah is special. I just think that his parents do not limit his expectations. In that situation Josiah, a one year old, faced a problem; came up with a solution; solved the problem; and continue on his merry way.

The only limits on black kids are those imposed by a sometimes racist society, or their parents. Josiah is now four years old with an insatiable curiosity and the ability to satisfy it. Let him go... let him grow.

School Choice

School choice refers to the practice of offering parents and students a variety of educational opportunities. Common choice options include magnet programs within the public school system, charter schools, and voucher programs. In the 1980s and 1990s, the "school choice movement" garnered significant attention from parents, educators, and policymakers seeking new methods of reforming public education. Public education reform is currently a foremost issue at the local, state, and national level.

Voucher Programs

Voucher programs award students all or part of their allocated public education funds to apply toward tuition at a private or public school of their choice. The label "voucher program" is encompassing. Included in the label are publicly and privately funded programs and, occasionally, tax-assistance or tax-credit options. Overall, students using voucher programs account for less than 1 percent of the national school-age population.

Whether voucher programs are successful in raising student achievement is a point of sometimes contentious debate and frequently depends upon the rigor of the study itself. Recent evaluations of voucher programs, including the Manhattan Institute's study of the Children's Scholarship Fund in Charlotte as well as studies of the New York, Dayton, and Washington D.C. privately-funded voucher programs, suggest that there are statistically significant achievement gains for low-income students, particularly African- American students, attending private schools through vouchers and scholarships. In Charlotte, for example, improvement gains after one year in attendance were between 5.4 and 7.7 percentile points for math and reading standardized scores.[2]

In Chicago, <u>Marva Collins</u>, an African American educator, created a low cost private school specifically for the purpose of teaching low income African American children whom the public school system had labeled as being "<u>learning disabled</u>." One article about Marva Collins' school stated, "Working with students having the worst of backgrounds, those who were working far below grade level, and even those who had been labeled as 'unteachable,' Marva was able to overcome the obstacles.

News of third grade students reading at ninth grade level, four-year-olds learning to read in only a few months, outstanding test scores, disappearance of behavioral problems, second-graders studying Shakespeare, and other incredible reports, astounded the public."[3]

During the 2006-2007 school year, Collins' school charged $5,500 for tuition, and parents said that the school did a much better job than the Chicago public school system. Meanwhile, during the 2007-2008 year, Chicago public school officials claimed that their budget of $11,300 per student was not enough. [4]

The Harlem Children Zone

The Harlem Children's Zone is a program that was profiled in a book by Paul Tough, Whatever It Takes. [5]

The Zone is the brainchild of Geoffrey Canada, an African American man in his mid-50s who grew up in extreme poverty in the South Bronx. Canada escaped the inner city for Bowdoin and Harvard and then returned to New York to try to create better options for kids like the ones he grew up with.

In the mid-'90s, he was running a decent-size nonprofit for teenagers in Harlem, where everyone told him how successful he was. But he could see only the kids he wasn't helping. Poor children in Harlem faced so many disadvantages, he realized, that it didn't make sense to address just one or two and ignore the rest. A great after-school program wouldn't do much good if the school itself were lousy. And even the best school would have a hard time succeeding without help from the parents.

Canada's solution was to take on all those problems simultaneously. The Harlem Children's Zone takes a holistic approach, following children from cradle to college, mimicking the cocoon of stimulation and support that surrounds middle-class children.

The Zone now enrolls more than 8,000 children a year in its various programs, which cover a 97-block section of central Harlem. "We're not interested in saving 100 kids," Canada told me once. "Even 300 kids, even 1,000 kids to me is not going to do it. We want to be able to talk about how you save kids by the tens of thousands, because that's how we're losing them. We're losing kids by the tens of thousands."[5]

Canada believes that many poor parents aren't doing enough to prepare their kids for school—not because they don't care, but because they simply don't know the importance of early childhood stimulation. So the Zone starts with Baby College, nine weeks of parenting classes that focus on discipline and brain development. It continues with language-intensive prekindergarten, which feeds into a rigorous K-12 charter school with an extended day and an extended year. That academic "conveyor belt," as Canada calls it, is supplemented by social programs: family counseling, a free health clinic, after-school tutoring, and a drop-in arts center for teenagers.

Canada's early childhood programs are in many ways a response to research showing that the vocabularies of poor children usually lag significantly behind those of middle-class children. At the Harlem Gems prekindergarten, four-year-olds were bombarded with books, stories, and flash cards—including some in French. The parents were enlisted, too; one morning, frequently families are take on a field trip to a local supermarket organized by the Harlem Children's Zone. The point wasn't to learn about nutrition, but rather about language—how to fill an everyday shopping trip with the kind of nonstop chatter that has become second nature to most upper-middle-class parents, full of questions about numbers and colors and letters and names. That chatter, social scientists have shown, has a huge effect on vocabulary and reading ability.[6] And as we walked through the aisles, those conversations were going on everywhere: Is the carrot bumpy or smooth? What color is that apple? How many should we buy?

So far, Canada's vision has yielded impressive results. Last year, the first conveyor-belt students reached the third grade and took their first statewide standardized tests. In reading, they scored above the New York City average, and in math they scored well above the state average.[7]

Obama's proposal is to replicate the Harlem Children's Zone in 20 cities across the country. In his speech announcing the plan, he proposed that each new zone operate as a 50-50 partnership between the federal government and local philanthropists, businesses, and governments, and he estimated that the federal share of the cost would come to "a few billion dollars a year." It's an undertaking that would mark a seismic change in the way that we approach poverty.[8]

ADOLESCENSE -THE CRAZY YEARS

Youthful mid-life crisis

It must be noted that I have no academic credentials to support the following views that I will offer. My views are those of a black male single parent of two boys and two girls.

The Same Sex Education Option

The Harlem Children's Zone primarily focuses on the early developing years of a child. Though critical in the development of young minds, we must not loose site of the equally critical stage of the middle years, the adolescent years, the crazy years. The adolescent years are the years of major distractions ie., identity crisis, and hormonal upheavals. It appears to have a more profound effect on the boys than girls, though the young female body is biologically changing also. The following are suggested as voluntary options within the school district for parents of kids during the crazy years.

There has been research documenting the performance of a Florida school that has separated some of its pupils.8 Kathy Piechura-Couture, Stetson University education professor said her research shows that separating boys and girls can be beneficial, although it's not a magic bullet.[9]

Her research found that the third year of a recent program, boys who attend class together tend to outperform boys in mixed classes in reading and math to a degree that is statistically significant. [10]

Girls also tend to do better, although the results aren't as consistent.[11]

Although the research is mixed, some studies suggest low-income children in urban schools learn better when separated from the opposite sex.[12] The concern about boys' performance in a secondary educational environment has also driven some of the interest in same-sex education. Socially, same-sex schools are emotionally easier on students. Stereotypes based on gender are not a huge issue in these settings. Girls are more outspoken and competitive when boys are not around to tease them. They also feel more comfortable participating in sports and other traditionally male dominated fields. [13]

Program like these should be strictly voluntary. They should start in the forth grade and end in the tenth grade.

The suggested starting grade gives a child the opportunity to become socially acclimated prior to reinforcing academic discipline. The ending grade also gives a socially insecure adolescent an opportunity to gain social self confidence. 14

The same sex environment offers the ideal opportunity for male/female mentoring. I have always been an advocate of adults participating in small group meals. Breakfast gives an adult the perfect opportunity to have open discussions on current events, social issues, and sometimes even personal problems. In most black families, this activity would never take place, because most black families don't have the luxury of time for this type activity due to work schedules. The mentoring aspect is so very important to adolescent kids, who in most instances grow up in single parent homes.

In 1990, only 9 percent of all children lived in single-parent households.[15] Presently in the United States, almost one third of children are born to single mothers.[16] A larger number of children will see their parents divorced before their eighteenth birthday.[17] Two third of black children are born out of wedlock.[18] Over half of American children will spend all or part of their childhood without their father in the home.[19] Same sex schools offer a unique opportunity for gender mentoring. These numbers indicate a pressing need for a race wide, structured mentoring program. The continued effort of mixed gender based education has not been successful for sectors of the young black male population- so why not try a voluntary based same sex program in select school systems?

"The definition of insanity is doing the same over and over while expecting a different results,"[20]

Military Academy Schools

Chicago has more student military programs than any city in the United States. In addition to the five schools, Chicago is home to 33 high school--based Junior Reserve Officer Training Corps(JROTC)programs. [21]

Supporters say that the programs teach kids discipline. Not everyone thinks these schools are a good idea, though. They say public schools shouldn't groom kids for the U.S. military under the guise of education. [22]

A BETTER FUTURE

Chicago's military high schools instill good work ethics and discipline in students, says the chief executive officer of the Chicago Public Schools, (now Secretary of Education)Arne Duncan. "[Military school is] getting these kids ready for college or whatever they want to do after high school. Our focus is just getting them as well prepared as we can ... for the rest of their lives," Duncan told Current Events. [23]

All but two of the schools--Chicago and Carver military academies--are too new to gauge how well they are performing, Duncan adds, but he's confident that they will turn out kids who score high on tests and go on to college. "[The graduation rate and test scores] are pretty good; they aren't as strong as we would like them to be, but they are going up," he says. Regardless, Duncan adds, demand from both parents and prospective students are high for the schools. Last year 7,500 applicants applied for the 700 freshman slots in the five schools.[24]

Others say Chicago's military schools and JROTC programs help average students thrive in school. "We intend to use the academies to take students who perform in the middle range and use the military model to enhance their ... education," Army Lt. Col. Rick Mills, who oversees the Chicago JROTC program, told the Chicago Tribune.[25]

TOO MUCH MILITARY

Those who oppose the schools and programs, however, think they are just ploys to get more kids into the military. "Chicago Public Schools should be in the business of educating children, not finding ways to indoctrinate them into the military," Brian Roa told the Chicago Tribune.[26] He's a Chicago science teacher who is a member of the National Network Opposing Militarization of Youth.

Darlene Gramigna of the American Friends Service Committee agrees. She says the schools' educational policies are too focused on the military. "So much of education has taken a military focus.... [In these schools] it's a different curriculum. It's the history of wars, and it's field trips to naval academies," Gramigna told Current Events.[27]

Kids don't need to practice countless drills to learn about discipline, Gramigna says. "I would like to believe that you could teach leadership and discipline in a variety of ways," she adds.[28]

Chicago Public Schools opened its fifth military high school in the fall of 2008--the Marine Military Academy. In 2009, a sixth school--an Air Force academy--will open as well. Chicago will be the only city with schools dedicated to the Army, Navy, Air Force, and Marines.

The National Defense Act of 1916 created the Junior Reserve Officer Training Corps (JROTC). Under the act, high schools receive federal funding and loans of military equipment as well as military instructors to provide three hours of military instruction per week. A school has to maintain at least 100 students over the age of 14 in the program.

The 1964 ROTC Vitalization Act expanded the program. About 500,000 students are involved in high school military programs across the United States, according to the Chicago Tribune.[29]

When a new military school opens in Chicago, it starts with only freshmen and then adds a new class each year.

AFTER SCHOOL PROGRAMS- A MISSED OPPORTUNITY

In too many schools today, 3 p.m. marks a daily missed opportunity to meet the tougher achievement demands placed on students and school districts.

For many children, it's when learning effectively stops and when opportunities for inappropriate behaviors line up to take their place. It's when many parents worry, rightly, that their children aren't sufficiently supervised. It's when community, youth, arts and law enforcement groups could /should become potential allies with the school district in assisting to maintain children on track and learning.

Ironically, it's the hour when many of the school district's investments in learning resources and facilities sit idle.

But in more and more school districts around the nation, it has become the time of day for new and creative learning opportunities, offered in settings where children are supervised by professional educators and community partners. By most assessments, today's after-school programs make a positive difference in the lives of students and improve the climate for school and district success.

Accordingly, after-school programs are very popular with the public. A series of annual voter surveys conducted by the Afterschool Alliance shows public support consistently running in the 90 percent range, with 76 percent of voters even going so far as to say they'd be willing to pay additional taxes if more after-school programs resulted.[30]

Multiple Effects

It is perhaps little surprising that those in the business of creating more after-school opportunities believe the current flat-lining of after-school funding is a very bad mistake. To advocates and practitioners, the benefits from after-school programs are in plain evidence, and study after study by independent academics have demonstrated their value. Researchers have examined the impact of programs on students' achievement, social interaction and safety. They've looked at short- and long-term effects. They've examined a broad variety of programs in a range of settings. Results vary somewhat from program to program, but the weight of the research evidence tells us that after-school, done right, lives up to its promise.

To hear Arne Duncan, than CEO of the Chicago Public Schools, (now Secretary of the Department of Education) tell it at a May 2003 press briefing: "If you look at results--and we do have to be bottom-line oriented--our test scores jumped to all-time highs, our mobility rate dropped to its lowest point ever, our truancy rate dropped to its lowest point ever, our graduation rate is at an all-time high.[31]

"For the first time ever, we have 8th graders beating national norms; that has never happened before. In a district where 85 percent of our students live below the poverty line, that was a huge real and symbolic accomplishment.

Children's minds don't stop at 3 p.m., and neither should their learning. So their schools and community partners should not stop teaching.[32]

According to the California Department of Education, an evaluation of the statewide found significant improvements in achievement among the most high-risk students," as well as "a direct relationship between gains in math and amount of participation in the program."[33]

Students who participated for 7.5 months or more demonstrated improvements in math scores that were more than 2.5 times those found statewide. School attendance also improved, especially among students having the highest number of absences prior to participating in the program.[34]

A Resource Question

Many school district leaders have found a solution to the funding problem in capitalizing on their own resources to leverage the involvement of community, law-enforcement, youth, parks and recreation, and faith, cultural and civic organizations to help sponsor and deliver quality after-school programs. District facilities, classrooms, computer and language labs, libraries, and arts and sports facilities keep students learning after 3 p.m.

Feed the Children

The most difficult time for large segments of the black population is after 3p.m, they will go to bed hungry. Sometime, for a lot of disadvantaged kids, the only meal that these kids will get is in school. It is impossible for a hungry kid to do homework assignments because they are hungry. The lucky kids attend a school that has a breakfast and lunch program. In most cases, they will get a snack in the morning, with lunch later. Often these are the only meals that they will get during the day. How can kids be developmentally productive when they are hungry?

There should be a commitment to, at the very lease, to provide an after school take- home meal for those kids who would like to have them. This is not rocket science, they provide lunches for prisoners with court appearances every day. The resources are already in place to accomplish this task through the school cafeteria staff present at most schools. It would only require increasing the food allotment at the relevant schools, and a possible increase of (1) additional staff. It is reasonable to realize an increase in student performance as result of this vital gesture. I know from personnel experience how important this would be to a lot of kids.

Teach Them Where They Live

Most disadvantaged kids live in or near housing clusters such as, housing projects, or apartment complexes. They are usually latchkey kids, with no parental supervision after 3p.m. They usually lack the necessary resources, (computers,) to complete take home assignments. A possible solution would be to set up learning centers in those complexes. The cost is the same for a basketball court, as it would be for a learning center. It would provide latchkey kids some place to go other than to an unsupervised home.

Research has proven that the more kids are supervised between 3p.m. and 6p.m., the lower the crime is in that given area. Consequently, a focused after-school program has multiple benefits for both community and student. The community realizes a reduction in counter productive behavior, and student realizes an increase in educational performance. That's a win win for both the student and the community.

Redefining the American High School

American high schools were not designed to prepare all of our young people to be successful citizens in today's challenging world.

The problem

Due to today's demanding job market, some kind of education after high school is vital—whether it's a four-year college, community college, technical school, or a formal apprenticeship. Yet most students leave high school without the necessary skills for college or a living wage job.

Nearly three out of 10 public high school students fail to graduate, and close to half of all African-American (44 percent) and Hispanic students (48 percent) leave high school without a diploma.[35]

Only 23 percent of African Americans and one-fifth of Hispanics graduate from high school prepared for a four-year college.[36]

Only three of five college freshmen will earn a B.A. within six years; for minority and low-income students, the number is closer to half.[37]

The consequences for the nation's civic and economic health

Nearly 40 percent of high school graduates feel inadequately prepared for college or the workplace.[38]

Colleges and employers are demanding the same core knowledge and skills.39 Over half of professors (54 percent) and nearly three-fifths of employers (58 percent) do not agree with the statement that high school graduates have the skills necessary for college or work respectively.[40]

The more education a person has, the more likely it is he or she will be employed.[41] Among high school dropouts ages 16 to 24, nearly half are jobless and a third receive some type of government assistance.[42]

Over a quarter (28 percent) of college freshmen must take remedial courses.[43]

By 2020, the nation may face a shortage of 14 million workers with college-level skills.[44]

High school dropouts will earn more than $1 million less over a lifetime than college graduates.[11]

Blacks have low educational attainment rates

There is an often repeated claim that "there are more black men in prison than in college." Besides being statistically wrong,[45] it also bolsters the second biggest myth about black Americans: it is a myth that blacks on the whole have low educational attainment rates. While there are statistics that point to less black men graduating college or lower college graduation rates. The absolute numbers of blacks attending college has increased over time and continues to increase.[46]

Historically Black Colleges and Universities (HBCUs) are institutions founded primarily for the education of African-Americans, although their charters were not exclusionary. Most HBCUs are 50 to 100 years old; the oldest HBCU dates back to 1837. Of the 105 HBCUs, 17 HBCUs have land-grant status. [47]

About 214,000 or 16 percent of all African-American higher education students in the nation are enrolled at HBCUs, which comprise 3 percent of all colleges and universities nation-wide. [48]

The National Association for Equal Opportunity in Higher Education (NAFEO) is a professional association that represents the nation's HBCUs.

Summary of Interesting Facts about HBCUs

Type Institution	No. of Institutions Per Type	Percent of Total HBCUs
4-Year Public	40	38.09%
4-Year Private	49	46.66%
2-Year Public	11	10.48%
2-Year Private	5	4.76%
Total	105	

HBCU African Americans Black Diamonds

Black Americans have a unique, yet undeveloped, educational opportunity to build an educated middle class in America. Through the proper managing, resourcing, and the demanding of education excellence the HBCU network can become a very special educational experience for black kids. Where else can you have the pride that results from watching the FAM marching band?

The HBCU network consists of 105 colleges and universities. Some are Land Grant; some are private, while others are state funded. In most instances they are underfunded and mismanaged. The management of these institutions is usually performed by educators, not business trained and experienced managers.

The academic credibility of some institutions is, in some instances, not competitive with most white institutions. This perception has been fostered by some in society with an agenda of diminishing the value of an education from HBCU. There is truth that Howard University is not competitive with Harvard University. The question that should be asked is, why? What ever the reason is, it should be resolved. There is now a cadre of skilled, experienced, professional black managers that should feel challenged to, after their current careers are over, help build one of the most valued black community resources, the HBCU system. There are former black CEO's of Fortune 500 companies that can bring a wealth of knowledge for setting up efficient management systems, financial resource development systems, and investment portfolio development. Recruiting retired senior corporate managers to form an HBCU management consulting structure for these institutions would began to bring some order.

For a variety of reasons, this resource has been allowed to fail many black kids. The problems are not always educational, they are mostly resource management. The HBCU system was, at one time, suppose to be exclusively for black kids. It was supposed to our place to educate our kids.

List of HBCU by State

ALABAMA
Alabama State University
Alabama A&M University
Tuskegee University

ARKANSAS
University of Arkansas Pine Bluff

DELAWARE
Delaware State University

DISTRICT OF COLUMBIA
Howard University

University of the District of Columbia

FLORIDA
Bethune Cookman College
Edward Waters
Florida A&M University

GEORGIA
Clark Atlanta University
Morehouse College
Morris Brown College
Spelman College

ILLINOIS
Malcolm X College

LOUISIANA
Grambling State University
Southern University

MARYLAND
Bowie State University
Coppin State College
Morgan State University
University of Maryland Eastern Shore

MISSISSIPPI
Alcorn State
Jackson State University
Tougaloo College

NORTH CAROLINA
Fayetteville State University
North Carolina A&T University
Saint Augustine College
Shaw University
Winston Salem State University

OHIO
Central State University

SOUTH CAROLINA
Claflin University

TEXAS
Prairie View A&M University
Texas Southern University

TENNESSEE
Fisk University
LeMoyne Owen College
Tennessee State University

VIRGINIA
Hampton University
Norfolk State University
Saint Paul College
Virginia State University

2

School-to-Career
Possible solution

THE CURRENT HIGH SCHOOL model is geared toward preparation for a college degree, with little emphasis on vocational skills training. Below is a copy of a Organized Labor brochure in support of School –to-Career program.
[1]

Get Connected to School-to-Career

This *Quick Guide* for Organized Labor is designed to help increase participation in School-to-Career efforts and to help you get started if you are not yet involved.

It provides teachers, employers, administrators, and other partners in School-to-Career an "inside look" on Labor's values and the roles we can play in local School-to-Career activities. Work is a big part of shaping who we are and how we contribute to our families and communities. Still, many of our young people leave school unprepared to enter the workforce and ill equipped to explore career options on their own. How can we best introduce young people to the opportunities of future careers and the contributions of organized labor? The School to Work Opportunities Act of 1994, backed by the AFL-CIO and teachers' unions, supports state and local partnerships of Labor, educators, employers, parents and community organizations to develop School-to-Career educational systems.

What is School-to-Career?

School-to-Career is an approach to education based on proven concepts. It is based on the idea that if students understand the relevancy of their academic studies and if their classroom learning is linked to future goals and careers, these students are likely to achieve higher performance in school and graduate with significantly improved knowledge and skills.

School-to-Career activities provide a better education for ALL students, whether they choose to attend college or move into the workforce. These activities may include curriculum enrichment (creating lessons that are current and relevant), worksite tours, classroom presentations on career and training opportunities, internships, and direct interaction with workers in real work situations. For those young people not fully engaged in their academic educational system, it encourages learning linked to future work and career efforts. This connection between the classroom and the world of work increase students' motivation and academic achievement, while better preparing our young people for their adult lives.

Why Should Labor Be Involved in School-to-Career?

Labor has been involved in School-to-Career (or School-to-Work) nationwide for many years. The logic is simple: we do the work and we are in the best position to share and pass on to younger people the "real stories" – life lessons about work places and relationships as well as the actual skills necessary to be successful in a particular career.

School-to-Career is an opportunity for union members to prepare the next generation for the world of work and help students explore a wide range of occupations and careers. We hope that many of these students will eventually become union brothers and sisters.

Organized Labor Makes Significant Contributions to Successful School-to-Career Systems

Organized Labor can be of substantial help in developing a comprehensive School-to-Career curriculum that conveys in a meaningful way all aspects of an industry showcasing those viewpoints of the workers performing the actual work. This might include the social interaction of work, the benefits of certain jobs, necessary skills for success and the long-term impact of working in a certain field.

Unions also operate apprenticeship training centers that offer preparation and hands-on learning to introduce students to the education, skills, and abilities needed to enter into registered trades and crafts apprenticeships. These apprenticeships require desire, certain aptitudes, a commitment of time, and considerable study but can all lead to high-wage, high-skill employment opportunities.

Additional contributions organized Labor makes to successful School-to-Career systems include:

Unions represent millions of front-line workers that can be called upon to support young people in job shadowing, mentoring, internships, apprenticeships and other work-based learning opportunities.

Unions have direct links to employers in a wide variety of occupational areas and can play a key role in facilitating employer involvement in School-to-Career activities.

Unions can play an important role in linking school-based learning with on-the-job training (OJT).

Unions are at the forefront of education and advocacy for workers' health and safety protection.

Unions can be instrumental in securing additional funding for local School-to-Career Partnerships and activities.

Organized Labor Benefits From Participation in School-to-Career

School-to-Career is a proven winner in education reform efforts. We have a self-interest as well as responsibility for providing young people with the best education possible; young people are the future of our Labor movement as well as society at large. By being active partners, we build stronger educational systems in our communities. As members of organized Labor, we expect every job to be done well and that the people performing the job are compensated fairly, work in a safe environment, and are treated with dignity and respect. Young people are well served to learn and understand our values. Labor's involvement in School-to-Career is an opportunity for us Through School-to-Career, Labor introduces an awareness of the contributions and to communicate this message directly.

The School-to-Work Opportunities Act: It's the Law...

It's important to know that statutes and laws mandate the inclusion of Labor in the design and implementation of School-to-Career systems. These laws provide safeguards for the rights of young workers in School-to-Career. These measures of inclusion and protection reinforce the important role Labor plays in the overall School-to-Career effort.

The School to Work Opportunities Act of 1994:

25 Highest-Paying Jobs for High School Grads

While nearly all of the highest paying jobs in America require a bachelor's degree or higher, good-paying occupations still exist that require only work experience or on-the-job-training.

Air traffic controllers had median hourly wages of $51.73 and median annual wages of $107,600 in 2005, making it the highest paid occupation that requires only work experience or on-the-job-training, according to the Bureau of Labor Statistics.

Air traffic controllers have seen their wages rise from 2005 to 2007. In July 2007, air traffic controllers earned a median of $120,842 in annual wages, according to HR.BLR.com's <u>Salary Center</u>.[2]

Among the 25 highest paid occupations overall, air traffic controller is the only one with no requirement for a bachelor's degree or higher.

Among occupations requiring only work experience or on-the-job-training, managers and industrial production managers are the second and third highest paying jobs.

The following are the 25 highest paying occupations requiring only work experience or on-the-job training:

	Occupation	Median Wages 2005	
		Hourly	Annual
1	Air Traffic Controllers	$51.73	$107,600
2	Managers, All Other	$38.06	$79,200
3	Industrial Production Managers	$36.34	$75,600
4	Transportation, Storage, and Distribution Managers	$33.23	$69,100
5	Nuclear Power Reactor Operators	$31.84	$66,200
6	First-Line Supervisors/Managers of Police and Detectives	$31.52	$65,600
7	First-Line Supervisors/Managers of Non-Retail Sales Workers	$29.79	$62,000
8	First-Line Supervisors/Managers of Fire Fighting and Prevention Workers	$29.25	$60,800
9	Sales Representatives, Wholesale and Manufacturing, Technical and Scientific Products	$29.21	$60,800
10	Gaming Managers	$28.82	$59,900
11	Elevator Installers and Repairers	$28.46	$59,200
12	Power Distributors and Dispatchers	$28.44	$59,200
13	Real Estate Brokers	$27.49	$57,200
14	Detectives and Criminal Investigators	$26.82	$55,800
15	Locomotive Engineers	$26.69	$55,500

16	Railroad Conductors and Yardmasters	$25.98	$54,000
17	Power Plant Operators	$25.56	$53,200
18	Postmasters and Mail Superintendents	$25.34	$52,700
19	Cost Estimators	$25.01	$52,000
20	First-Line Supervisors/Managers of Mechanics, Installers, and Repairers	$24.99	$52,000
21	First-Line Supervisors/Managers of Construction Trades and Extraction Workers	$24.98	$52,000
22	Gas Plant Operators	$24.96	$51,900
23	Petroleum Pump System Operators, Refinery Operators, and Gaugers	$24.55	$51,100
24	Captains, Mates, and Pilots of Water Vessels	$24.49	$50,900
	Telecommunications Equipment Installers and Repairers	$24.33	$50,600

On a daily basis young students in America are bombarded with the notion that you can only succeed in life if you have a post secondary education. To reinforce this notion, the educational system is primarily structured to accomplishing this goal. President Barack Obama, when speaking on education, constantly reinforces college as the only road to success in life. Those without the financial resource or the GPA are given few career options. In most instances, they give up because they have no interest in college. They are never told of, or prepared for all of the other great options out there such as vocational and technical career options.

In the earlier example of school to career, if properly executed, every student would have a path to becoming a productive, responsible adult after high school .and, In many cases a college degree will become a viable later option because of financial stability. All of the previously mentioned jobs are export proof. These are infrastructure related, and can only be performed by the local labor force. These positions are also relative free of the fluctuations in the financial cycles. Subsequently, these education and career option should be made available to future students.

That option and dream in today's environment is crushed, leaving only frustration, bad choices, and bad outcomes. The world might be designed by scholars, but it is built by technicians. Everyone should have a dream.

3

BLACK WEALTH

THE TRUE STORY OF *wealth in the Black Community*

"*The recent economic downturn was the result of banks being forced to make risky loans to African Americans.*" *This was the propaganda repeated daily, mostly on cable media. Cable TV would have you believe that over reaching of poor black folk, with little ability to pay a mortgage, created the financial crisis that almost destroyed the world's banking system.*

Nothing could have been father from the truth. The world financial crisis was the outgrowth of greed and opportunity taken by unregulated real estate and financial institutions in the USA.

Some in the media would have you believe that real estate loan defaults made to African Americans created the collapse in the stock market. Nothing could have been father from the truth. The areas with the highest default rates had the smallest black population ie., Miami, Las Vegas, Orlando, Phoenix, and Riverside. These areas do not have high concentrations of African American populations.[1]

The vehicle for the fraud was sub-prime loans. There are two types of cases where someone gets a subprime loan. In the first of the two scenarios, a person who already owns a home wants to refinance the mortgage in order to make significant repairs to the home.

In the second scenario, someone is trying to buy a first home. Eager to achieve such a milestone, the buyer neglects to study carefully the conditions of the loan being offered.

Unscrupulous mortgage brokers and the lending industry preyed on both groups of people. But homeowners and first-time homebuyers with good credit became the victims of predatory lending as well, said Cathy Mickens of Neighborhood Housing Services in Jamaica, Queens. [2]

"It has spread throughout the community," Mickens said, affecting middle-income and high-income people as well as those with lower incomes. Some people who could have gone to a conventional lender and qualified for a standard mortgage will instead go to a predatory lender who promises to provide the loan quickly and with no documents required. Often, Mickens said, the result is "a disaster." [3]

Who Is to Blame?

While some have suggested that borrowers are at fault because of their zeal to own a home, or get-quick money, unscrupulous mortgage brokers, lending institutions and Wall Street investors, motivated by greed and racism, are the driving forces. The result was a financial predatory attack on black wealth.

(April 18, 2005) A recent report issued by the Boston College Center on Wealth and Philanthropy (CWP) projects that the wealth transfer from African-American households via estates in the 55-year period between 2001 and 2055 will range between $1.1 trillion to $3.4 trillion (in 2003 U.S. dollars). [4]

It was found that the growth in wealth among younger African-Americans who grew up after civil rights legislation was in effect identical to that for Caucasians of the same age and this is a hopeful sign for African-American wealth in the future," said CWP Associate Director John Havens, who directed the study.[5]

Warmed-over Myths of Black Wealth

Newsflash from CNBC's NEWBOs: If you're black and can't rap or play ball, forget about making it in America.

By Alfred Edmond, Jr. - February 27,

2009

It's 2009 and a black man is President of the United States of America. So why is CNBC still programming like its 1989 and the only way black Americans can hope to achieve wealth is via a sports contract or a record deal? CNBC's <u>NEWBOs: The Rise of America's New Black Over Class</u>, a special which aired recently[6] is wrong on so many levels.

But its biggest disservice is that it is based on two stereotypical myths about black wealth that are just not supported by the facts that: The best—and even the only—avenue to real wealth for black Americans are through sports and entertainment.

The majority of the "NEWBOs" featured on the program hit, run and jump for a living (the NFL's Terrell Owens, Major League Baseball's Torii Hunter and the NBA's LeBron James) or perform on stage and recordings (Cash Money Records co-partner and rapper Bryan "Baby" Williams, contemporary gospel artist Kirk Franklin).

An exception is RLJ Development CEO and billionaire Robert L. Johnson—the only subject featured who can make a credible claim to being "uber-wealthy." Of course, he made his fortune by creating and marketing a cable channel featuring black people singing, dancing and rapping. (Oh, and unless you're Oprah Winfrey, black women need not apply—apparently there are no female NEWBOs.)

Black athletes and entertainers are among the richest black Americans and among the nation's wealthiest Americans.

The problem with this is that NEWBOs primarily focuses on the gross income of the subjects. However, the real measure of wealth is not gross income, but net worth—a person's assets minus their liabilities.

(Black Enterprise readers are familiar with the net worth tables accompanying the monthly Wealth for Life profiles.) Lee Hawkins, the host/interviewer of NEWBOs and a Wall Street Journal reporter who's authored a forthcoming book about this group, goes to great pains to hype the fact that "black athletes in the NFL, NBA and Major League Baseball and the 20 highest paid hip-hop entrepreneurs" earn a combined total of $4.5 billion dollars. He quickly moves past the fact that this is the combined income of more than 1,000 people, and never mentions that the combined net worth—the real wealth—of this group would be a small fraction of that total.

Athletes and entertainers earn good money—but they don't even come close to being uber-wealthy, the term Hawkins repeatedly uses without ever defining what he actually means when he says it.[7]

Aren't these the stereotypes and false massagers we've spent much of the past 40 years trying to deprogram from American thinking, and black American thinking in particular?

In the age of Obama, why are we still telling each other—and worse, our children—that our best chance to become wealthy in America is through sports and entertainment? Especially when anyone who understands wealth and the

American economy, as CNBC and Hawkins surely do, know that is not true?

Ken Fisher's book <u>The Ten Roads to Riches: The Way the Wealthy Got There (And How You Can Too!)</u>, correctly identifies sports and entertainment as the most difficult way to achieve serious wealth, with the longest odds. The primary reasons to pursue a career in sports or entertainment is because you are good at it, and you like to do it—not because you have more than a prayer of ending up with Bob Johnson money.

There are no athletes or entertainers on the most recent <u>Forbes 400 list of the wealthiest Americans</u>. (You needed a net worth of at least $1.3 billion to make the most recent list. Their combined net worth is $1.57 trillion.) It's extremely rare for a recording artist or athlete to maintain his or her earning power past the age of 35.[8]

To identify the wealthiest black Americans would take a lot of digging—after all, truly wealthy black people, (including many of the corporate CEOs, Wall Street executives and owners of Black Enterprise 100s companies featured in Black Enterprise) are not eager to draw attention to their wealth.

African American Wealth

by Susan Anderson

From Mark Twain's Pudd'nhead Wilson to television's George Jefferson, wealthy African Americans are seldom accepted on their own terms. When not satirized in the *media, they are frequently portrayed as "sell-outs" who "make it" by turning their backs on their own. This negative attitude is partly traceable to sociologist E. Franklin Frazier's seminal "Black Bourgeoisie: The Rise of a New Middle Class." In his 1957 study, Frazier, himself African American, accused wealthy blacks of accepting, "unconditionally, the values of the white bourgeois world" because "they do not truly identify themselves with Negroes." Even this year's publication of "Our Kind of People: Inside America's Black Upper Class," by Lawrence Otis Graham, inadvertently reinforces Frazier's attitude by focusing on superficial details of some black elite: lavish homes, parties and exclusive clubs.*

In Los Angeles, notions about upper-class blacks can be especially misleading. Here the words "black wealth" usually conjure up images of professional athletes and movie stars. It doesn't help that former Lakers Earvin "Magic" Johnson, owner of Johnson Development Corp., makes headlines with every business deal. But while you may not have sipped coffee at the La Tijeras Plaza Starbucks, in which Johnson has a stake, or seen a film at the Magic Johnson Theatres at the Baldwin Hills Crenshaw Plaza, you have probably relied, at one time or another, on a Thomas Guide. When Warren B. Wilson, an African American entrepreneur, retired and sold Thomas Bros. Maps to Rand McNally earlier this year, he was sole proprietor of the 200-employee firm with annual sales of $25 million.

The easy focus on celebrity money, ignorance of the long history of black enterprise and lingering skepticism about the racial loyalties of rich black folks--all combine to obscure the truth about black wealth and business ownership in Southern California.

To most people, black business means mom and pop stores, barbecue stands and barber shops located in the 'hood. These businesses certainly contribute to individual prosperity and neighborhood economies, as well as to local culture. Central Avenue, in its heyday of African American life, represented this kind of vitality. Today, the shops, art galleries, jazz clubs and small merchants located in Leimert Park also offer evidence of a thriving community, in which employment, home ownership and incomes are stable and high.

But the largest black-owned companies aren't to be found in historically black neighborhoods. Instead, they are spread around Los Angeles--in the South Bay, the financial district, in beach communities, downtown and in manufacturing zones. Black entrepreneurs are in high-tech, garment manufacturing, personal services, aluminum processing and distribution, and aerospace. Los Angeles is the only metropolitan area with three sizable black-owned banks; African Americans own and operate construction-equipment suppliers, major auto dealerships, architecture firms, art galleries and insurance and realty firms. L.A. is also home to the "granddaddy" of large black U.S. companies, C.H. James and Son, Inc., established in 1883.

The fact is, more high-income blacks live in Los Angeles County than anywhere else. There are a growing number of them who own businesses and assets that comprise real wealth. The most recent Census figures show that there are 32,645 black-owned businesses in the county, with total revenue of more that $3.6 billion and 25,082 employees.

These companies are run by African American entrepreneurs who not only successfully compete in the open market and create wealth, but also give back to their communities. The range of their community, civic and charitable involvement is wide. According to Patricia Means, publisher of Turning Point magazine and a member of the board of the Jenessee Center shelter for battered women and children, these entrepreneurs exhibit "a commitment to not only do good for [themselves], but to do good for the community. It comes from tradition. We have been taught to reach back and help somebody. You're not successful if you don't."

They are living proof that Frazier's generalizations about the black bourgeoisie are outdated.

Compared with other companies, a study by the Joint Center for Political and Economic Studies shows, black businesses "were more likely to participate in programs to assist young people, welfare recipients and individuals from high-poverty neighborhoods." Indeed, a distinguishing mark of many black-owned companies is a dedication to diversity in their work forces. For example, out of 40 employees at Bazile Metals Service, with annual sales of $15 million, 60% are African American, 35% Latino and 5% white. President Barry Bazile also operates Welfare to Work Partners, a nonprofit that provides education, training and jobs for low-income participants.

Many blacks were first-time owners in their industry and are eager to find ways to keep the doors open for those who follow them. Carl Burhanan, owner of Oasis Aviation, aspires to grow his Marina del Rey-based fuel-supply business from current sales of $41.3 million to $100 million. Yet, aware of his own experiences of racism inside and outside the military, Burhanan helped found the 300-member U.S. Army Black Aviation Assn., which gives scholarships to African American students who want to pursue an aviation career.

Education is a high priority for socially conscious black entrepreneurs. Clarissa Faye Howard, owner of Bd Systems, offers internships for inner-city youth at her $40-million-a-year firm. The founder of the $80-million Act 1 Personnel Services, Janice Bryant Howroyd, funds scholarships for students attending historically black colleges, company internships and, in conjunction with The Links, an exclusive black women's club, works on a mentoring program, Project Life, for low-income youths in Carson schools. Eric Hanks, who grosses $1 million in annual sales as owner of M. Hanks Gallery, teaches affordable classes on art appreciation and speaks regularly at public schools. Karl Kani, whose company employs 45 and takes in $69 million in annual sales, serves on the advisory board of the Mayor's after-school enrichment program, L.A.'s Best.

Black businesses' emphasis on "giving back" flows from fresh memories of discrimination and the knowledge that the history of race in America is in part one of the economic subordination of black people, beginning with slavery and continuing, after Reconstruction, with the exclusion of blacks from certain occupations and professions. Black business owners like Henry O'Bryant, who began in the 1950s by manufacturing uniforms for once-fledgling companies like McDonald's, recalls being told at the Frank Wiggins Trade School that tailoring classes were "reserved for white kids." Broadway Federal Bank, with $139.5 million in assets and $119 million in deposits, was established in 1946 by H. Claude Hudson, dentist and Los Angeles NAACP founder, to satisfy the post-World War II demand for homeownership when black GIs were denied mortgages by mainstream banks.

L.A.'s black business owners, however, tend not to harbor anger over the inequities of the past or present. They are more likely to exhibit the faith of Biddy Mason. Mason, a former slave, built a fortune in downtown real estate and nursing homes before her death in 1891. In addition to her business acumen, she founded a church and was a philanthropist and political agitator. Mason taught that, "If you hold your hand closed, nothing good can come in. The open hand is blessed, for it gives in abundance, even as it receives."

Political debate among blacks still makes much of the contentious rift between Booker T. Washington and W.E.B. Du Bois over which road leads to freedom. Du Bois, a founder of the National Assn. for the Advancement of Colored People, criticized Washington, president of Tuskegee Institute, for embracing black capitalism and shying away from what he considered to be necessary political engagement on behalf of full rights for all blacks. What few know is that the idea for Washington's premiere organization, the National Negro Business League, founded in 1900, came from Du Bois. It was

Du Bois who organized the university conference at which he proposed the federation of local businesses that would enable black people to join "the industrial and mercantile spirit of the age."

If generating economic power means stronger black representation in society and politics, there is obviously scant cause for scoffing at black wealth. African American entrepreneurs face the same challenges as other business owners, and then some. They battle traces of historical discrimination, a lack of available capital and the tough competition that marks the huge, diverse L.A. market, the biggest business base in the country. Here, where the African American population has always been proportionately low, black-owned businesses are vastly outnumbered not only by those owned by whites, but also by those run by Latinos and Asian Americans.

Given history's shameful determination to limit black economic independence, African American entrepreneurs have a unique story to share about the arc of success. But their real success lies in a near-universal commitment to community and civic service. Theirs is a corporate model worth emulating.

Oprah Winfrey tops the inaugural Forbes list of the Wealthiest Black Americans, as well as being the wealthiest self-made woman.

Oprah Winfrey is one of the most lucrative brands in the world. Today the Oprah Winfrey Show airs in 144 countries, drawing 44 million U.S. viewers each week. Her Harpo Productions helped create the likes of Dr. Phil and Rachael

Ray. She's produced Broadway shows and has her own satellite radio channel. For all of this, she consistently earns more than $200 million a year.

And unlike many others on our list, her business is weathering the recession well. Winfrey continues to entice viewers with money-saving tips, celebrity interviews and relationship advice. She's debuting a new show this fall, which will be hosted by frequent guest Dr. Oz, and is planning to launch The Oprah Winfrey Network early next year.

With a net worth of $2.7 billion, Winfrey tops the inaugural Forbes list of the Wealthiest Black Americans. She is the only billionaire on the list of 20 tycoons, all of whom are self-made. The group built their fortunes across a spectrum of industries spanning athletics and entertainment, media, investments, real estate, construction and restaurants.

Black Entertainment Television founder Robert Johnson became the first African American billionaire in 2000 after he sold the network to Viacom (VIA - news - people) for $3 billion in stock and assumed debt. Since then, sagging Viacom and CBS (CBS - news - people) stock, plus investments in real estate, hotels and banks--industries pummeled in the past year amid the recession--have dragged Johnson's net worth to $550 million, we estimate. He ranks third on the list; his former wife and BET co-founder, Sheila Johnson, ranks seventh with $400 million.

Wealthiest African-Americans

The following list is the ranking of America's richest Black Americans on May 6, 2009.

Wealthiest African-Americans

#	Name	Net worth (USD)	Residence	Sources of wealth
1	Oprah Winfrey	$2.7 billion	Illinois	Harpo Productions
2	Tiger Woods	$600 million	Florida	Golf, endorsements
3	Robert Johnson	$550 million	Florida	BET, hotel investments
4	Michael Jordan	$525 million	Illinois	Basketball, Nike, endorsements
5	Earvin "Magic" Johnson, Jr.	$500 million	California	Basketball, real estate, investments
6	William Henry Cosby, Jr.	$450 million	Massachusetts	The Cosby Show, entertainment
7	Sheila Johnson	$400 million	Virginia	BET, investments
8	R. Donahue Peebles	$350 million	Florida	Real estate
9	Berry Gordy, Jr.	$325 million	California	Motown Records, Jobete Records
10	Quintin Primo III	$300 million	Illinois	Real estate

11	*Don King*	*$290 million*	✕ *Florida*	Boxing, Promotions
12	*Janice Bryant Howroyd & family*	*$250 million*	▲ *California*	Staffing, Investments
13	*Herman J. Russell*	*$200 million*	*Georgia (U.S. state)*	Construction, real estate
14	*Ulysses Bridgeman, Jr.*	*$200 million*	*Georgia (U.S. state)*	Restaurants
15	*Tracy Maitland*	*$150 million*	*Kentucky*	Investments
16	*Alphonse Fletcher, Jr.*	*$150 million*	*New York*	Investments
17	*Shawn "Jay-Z" Carter*	*$150 million*	*New York*	Rocawear, Entertainment, investments
18	*Kobe Bryant*	*$140 million*	▲ *California*	Basketball, endorsements
19	*Shaquille O'Neal*	*$130 million*	*Arizona*	Basketball, endorsements
20	*Kenneth I. Chenault*	*$125 million*	*New York*	American Express

Blacks are economically depressed

Another common misperception of African-Americans is that on the whole, blacks are economically depressed or poor in the United States. Once again, media crime reports from the 'ghetto,' hip-hop videos and gangsta rap do not show an accurate picture of black American wealth as a whole.

There is a projection that based on purchasing power alone, African-Americans eclipse all African countries and many emerging countries. African-American purchasing power is projected to <u>exceed $1 trillion by 2012</u>. This figure outstrips most other countries <u>GDP</u>. In fact, if African Americans were a country, it would be the tenth largest economy in the world today.[9]

The numerous portrayals in the mainstream media of black poverty and the seemingly "permanent" underclass do not reflect the overall wealth of African-Americans in the USA.

If the African-American portion of the US GDP was separated from the rest of the US GDP, <u>its $688 Billion</u> would still eclipse most Third World and indeed many other "developed" countries, including Sweden.[10]

Not too many countries can match this amount, and blacks only have 13% of the US population.

Many other countries make do with less GDP, and with many more people. The true test for the future is the effective use of this massive wealth to achieve proper respect.

4

THE NEW POLITICS IN AMERICA
THE AWAKENING

THE RECENT ELECTION OF *Barack Obama as president of the United States signaled an awakening of black folk in America. The African American voting population, until the recent election for president, was ignored by republicans, and courted only in a close election by democrats. This was a tactic designed by politicians to control black voters for their vote, while minimizing their influence or rewards after an election. The recent threat of a Blackout (blacks refusing to vote en mass) in the general election sent shockwaves throughout the Democratic Party before the presidential election of 2008.*

The election of Barack Obama was important to black America's pride, but far more important was the message: that the Democrats can not elect a president without the black vote.

From this day forward, African Americans should understand the value and power of their vote. They must have a well thought out agenda to improve their lives through their vote. Blacks now know that they have true political value; the challenge is to use it wisely Forty years of wandering in the political wilderness was required to get to this level. Cable political analysis Pat Buchanan has predicted black complacency in the 2010/2012 elections.

During the early presidential campaign, Obama was never really seriously considered a viable candidate, not by white America, nor black America. Most of white America was not yet ready for a black president, and blacks dared not dream. So whites scoffed and blacks reluctantly supported Hillary.

I was always amazed at the media's image of Obama's campaign as being Barack and Michelle sitting around a dirty kitchen table counting twenty dollar donations from poor black folks.

The perception that the media pushed was a campaign managed and run by the local civic association. Nothing could have been father from the truth.

After his victory in Iowa some black folk dared to dream, while others supported Hillary. The media ravaged Hillary after Iowa, creating a white backlash vote in New Hampshire.

It was the New Hampshire win, and the subsequent "Jessie Jackson "statement by Bill Clinton after Obama's victory in South Carolina that created the black awakening. Blacks accounted for a majority of democratic voters in South Carolina, 55 percent -- the highest turnout among African-Americans in any Democratic presidential primary for which data are available. And a huge proportion of them, 78 percent, supported Obama, compared with 19 percent for Hillary Clinton and just 2 percent for John Edwards.[1]

After the South Carolina win by Obama and Bill Clinton's "Jessie Jackson" reference, CNN's Dona Brazil expressed her outrage and coined the term, "Blackout" meaning that in November blacks would stay away from the poles if the election was unfairly stolen from Obama. The Democratic Party knew that that would doom any chance of electing any democrat as president.

Something emerged after the South Carolina primary was that the Obama campaign was for real. It was superbly financed: tactically and strategically in its thinking and planning. In an article by Robert Schlesinger it was pointed out how important the black vote was in the primaries, but wasn't quite sure about the general election.[2] I think that some knew that they would have a tremendous effect on the general election based on the demographics of the Electoral College. The black demographics proved to be critical in the Obama general election strategy just as some analysts knew that the old strategy was no longer valid.

Electoral College votes won the presidency. There were many states that had large concentrations of African Americans who will forever in the future affect the Electoral College. The following article proves the point.

Do Democrats need the black vote?

By Robert Schlesinger

How much do black voters matter to Democrats in a presidential election? Try 76 electoral votes worth.

I was home in NYC for part of Easter weekend and during a family gathering, the Democratic debate broke out. My family reflects the current Democratic spectrum: We've got a staunch Obama-ite (who would not vote for Clinton), a couple of either-works-for-me types (including me), some committed Clinton-ites (at least one of whom swears they will not pull the lever for Obama in November).

I argued that Barack Obama's got the nomination virtually sewn up, barring a colossal collapse. She can't overtake him in pledged delegates, and the super delegates (being mostly elected officials who have to stand on a Democratic ticket in the fall and in the future) won't risk the wrath of black voters by tossing Obama aside.

One of my brothers raised an objection I had not heard before: Black voters are critical in Democratic primaries, he argued, because they make up a huge portion of the electorate, especially in the south; but in how many general election states *is the black vote important for Democrats? I didn't have an answer. Thanks to exit polls and some rough calculations, I now do.*

I started with the 20 states that John Kerry won in 2000; then using CNN's exit polls I estimated the number of black voters in each state and the number that voted Democratic. I found that black votes numbered more than Kerry's margin for error in six states: Pennsylvania (21 electoral votes), Michigan (17), New Jersey (15), Maryland (10), Wisconsin (10), and Delaware (3).

Of course there's no scenario under which black voters simply don't show up. Instead, the danger is depressed turn-out. So, again using CNN's exit poll numbers, I ran some estimates of what would happen if a smaller percentage of blacks turned out:

- At 90 percent black turn-out, Wisconsin's 10 electoral votes slide into the GOP column.

- At 75 percent black turn-out, Pennsylvania's 21 electoral votes go Republican.

- At 70 percent Michigan's 17 electoral votes turn from blue to red.

- At 50 percent the GOP collects Delaware's three electoral votes.

I don't know what a realistic number to project is for the effects of angry black apathy, but I'll stop at 50 percent. It may be that going as low as 75 percent is unrealistic. Most likely it's impossible to say. (And this doesn't take into account things like congressional districts where black voters make the margin of difference.)

The aforementioned statistics should validate the value of black voters for national elections in the future. Complacency is no longer an option for black voters. Don't repeat the lesson of the post Jessie Jackson presidential run in the 80's, in which frustration over Jessie's unsuccessful run caused an opting out of the political process. This ultimately caused the black vote to be rendered valueless except in close races.

The recent 85% turnout established the true power of the black electorate.

5

THE NEXT GENERATION

THE FORTY YEAR TREK *by African Americans through the economic and political wilderness was lead by the old warriors. They are now tired and deserving of the right to stand down. They are the warriors from the MLK Regiment who fought, and yes sometimes died to insure that all of those who followed would have the opportunity to be free of the Curse of Willie Lynch.*

The MLK Regiment, manned by Jessie Jackson, Meager Evers, Malcolm X, John Lewis, Ron Dellums, Shirley Chisholm, Barbara Jordan, Al Sharpton, etc.,, sat-in, demonstrated, and protested with the hope that the next generation would not have to.

The next generation of black leadership must understand that true power in America is manifested in three ways; 1. Political power- -the power of the voting block; 2.Economic power- the ability to create and control wealth; 3. Family- the cornerstone of any society, from which flow the understanding of education, moral values, and a since of self.

Politics-The True Black Power- the vote

Forty years ago religiously educated men were sent by African Americans to congress to compete with lawyers.

Today we send lawyers to compete with lawyers. In the beginning we would ask (sometimes beg) for a place at the table of power. Today, because of our political power, demonstrated in the recent presidential election, we are invited, no implored, to participate.

Today we hold the balance of power for the election of the Democratic candidate for President provided that we continue to function in the same way as the African American voting bloc that decided the 2008 election.

Because of our unified participation in that election the first African American, Barack Obama, was elected president of the United States.-- Martin was proud...

During the journey, we either did not participate in the national political process, or our participation was so fragmented that it garnered very little respect, though it probably should be mentioned that the voting rights bills contributed significantly to black American enfranchisement during the journey)

Now, especially after the recent presidential election, we understand the need to be united. The need now is to develop a meaningful future agenda.

We must strive to understand our needs as a race of people in this society to bring about meaningful changes in our lives.

In the past, black folks would get to the mountain top, but could never get over. Today you have elected a president.….. We must never again become complacent with our vote. In the future politicians should earn our vote, not take us for granted.

Wealth building

Wealth is the ability to afford both the necessities and the pleasures of life. More important, wealth is the vehicle for demanding respect.

The present generation has amassed a trillion dollars in GDP wealth. There need to be an appreciation for the value and leverage of such wealth.

In the past, when we were offended in the market place, we would feel distressed but would continue to shop at that establishment due to limit options. In past banks would take our money but would refuse to loan us our own money.

Red Lining was used in the real estate and mortgage industries to create BLACK RESIDENTIAL ZONES. Now the industry will enable you to live anywhere you want for a price. Now the term for Black Mortgages is "Sub-prime".

Sub-prime is the mortgage that almost brought about the collapse of the world wide financial markets. The mortgage was designed to provide high interest mortgages to high risk borrowers. They were only suppose to be applied to high risk borrowers, instead unscrupulous real estate agents and mortgage brokers saw an opportunity to profit off unsophisticated minority borrowers. In most cases dreamers were sold homes of their dreams; the problem was that they could not afford the monthly notes that eventually reset to higher monthly notes. Everybody profited except the home owners who eventually lost their homes.

This point is worth mentioning because we must educate black society to recognize those types of frauds. We must also punish those in the real estate and mortgage industries who would participate in such practices, by identifying the perpetrators and withholding all future business. (One trillion GDP) An organized effort like that would send shockwaves throughout the financial sector in America. Demand the respect- withhold your money.

The Greeks are the new Elders

Societies function off internal structures which give them order, and networks to provide immediate communication.

College fraternities and sororities provide existing structures for both leadership and communication. Because they are usually nation wide, they can provide a closed communication loop for both ideas and issues, coast to coast. Such capacity would make it possible to warn someone in San Francisco of a problem that occurred in Hampton Virginia almost immediately.

The more important role of the Greek Elders would be to provide mentors for the youngsters, both boys and girls. They could provide a moral framework; a value system; and a successful adult image for developing minds.

It is your turn to step up. Give up one Happy Hour for a black child.

Other examples of the new elders appeared in a recent CNN Special – In Black In America2- produced by Solidad O'Brian, there are some prime examples of the new elders:

Malaak Compton Rock: (wife of comedian Chris Rock) was an active participant in sponsoring a trip for 65 black and Hispanic kids to South Africa. The trip proved to be life changing for some of the kids.

Tyler Perry: Tyler Perry is the first African-American to own a major film and TV studio

The director, writer and playwright grew up poor in New Orleans, Louisiana

Perry's movies have grossed nearly $400 million; he's developed a loyal following

"[If] this little boy from Louisiana can do it, anybody can do it," says Perry

Tyler Perry is cited because of his response to a situation in Philadelphia, Pa. where black kids were refused admission to a privately owned swimming pool. The kids were devastated. Tyler Perry's response was to sponsor an all expense paid trip to Disney World.

Steve Perry: Principal Steve Perry founded the school to serve kids with backgrounds like his- Capital Prep Magnet School in Hartford, Connecticut, sends every graduate to college. Capital Prep boasts a near zero dropout rate; Perry sets the highest of expectations

Perry's demanding approach has yielded significant results. The school of just under 300 sixth- through 12th-grade students boasts a near 0 percent dropout rate. That's a stunning achievement considering Hartford is one of the lowest performing districts in Connecticut, a state with one of the largest achievement gaps between black and white students in the nation.

According to the Connecticut Coalition for Achievement NOW, an educational advocacy group, black students in Connecticut are, on average, three grade levels behind their white peers.[2]

Capital Prep, a year-round school that is more than 80 percent black and Latino, can boast of sending every graduating member of its senior class on to a four-year college. In the four years since Perry founded the school, he has sent 80 students on to college.

6

The Power of Money

THE AFRICAN AMERICAN COMMUNITIES *control a wealth in Gross Domestic Product (GDP) of one trillion dollars. Such spending power should warrant some level of respect. The fact that this has not occurred is due to the lack of sophisticated leveraging of money for respect by African Americans.*

In Dr. King's Memphis speech, he suggested the use of organized boycotting of racially offensive businesses as a means of demanding respect. The key to a successful boycott is unity of purpose.

It is always distressing to watch interviews with black folk complaining about treatment of a particular business. The frustration that they feel is expressed sometimes with aggression, and more often with a sense of impotence. Such expressions are more the result of a lack of understanding that they influence the future of that business. It's not even necessary to discuss the offensive behavior with the business; just discontinue supporting the business. I doesn't matter weather it's Wal-Mart, General Motors, or Yums carry out. You don't have to ask for respect, they will understand very quickly, and will change their behavior. No one will disrespect African Americans when they learn to leverage their wealth.

The media is not exempt from such a boycott. Recently there was an interesting experience during the presidential campaign relative to the TV media. A fan of political talk shows; one in particular, Morning Joe on MSNBC had a regular participant named Pat Buchanan, a person of strong racist views felt no constraints on what he would say. The show and the network thought it was particularly entertaining for him to make his insensitive, vile remarks, until a black viewer complained to the show's sponsors with the threat that African Americans would discontinue purchasing their products if it continued.

The very next day Pat was conspicuously absent. He remained absent for the rest of the week. When he returned, his rhetoric had toned down, though not for long. No major demonstration: just an email.

The life blood of any media is sponsorship. Any sponsor will not risk loosing market share if it thinks that a particular show, that they sponsor, is offensive to any segment of their market. Black folk should not fail to voice displeasure with any sector of society that it views as offensive or non-responsive. A quiet, yet organized collective response is extremely effective. Or just stop spending your money.

7

It Takes a Village

Over the past forty years black families have had to endure a planned assault on the cornerstone of any society, the family.

Prior to the beginning of the civil rights movement of the early sixties, black families remained a traditional social unit, with a father, mother, and children. There was also a supportive extended family structure. The stability of this social structure created endured through pre-Great Society. The stability of this structure created a challenge to whites with limited education and vocational training because it created competition in the job market for the same jobs.

It is important to give some historical perspective to the previous statement.

The end of the Civil War placed plantation owners in a position of having to negotiate with their previously owned slaves to harvest their croups. It also put poor whites in a position of having to compete with former slaves for work. This was intolerable, thus over time, the imbalance was addressed through a series of legal actions called the Black Codes, with ultimate illegal but unchallenged enforcement through the use of the KKK. Thus began the one hundred year journey to the beginning of the Civil Rights Movement of the nineteen sixties.

White society was not inclined to repeat the post Civil War experience. An effective way of dealing with the problem had to be found.

The most effective way to deal with the problem came with the introduction of welfare

It would be hard to attribute a premeditated mindset to the destructive affects of programs of the Great Society. Yet the ultimate effects have taken forty years to recover from. Pre-Civil War slavery was instituted to build wealth for those select few in white society through the free labor of slaves. Some programs of the civil rights era were design to protect wealth from competitive blacks through destruction of initiative.

Welfare was one of those tools. In the nineteen sixties white saw history repeating itself. Instead of the Black Codes, the new weapon was an assault on the family structure through the use of welfare. This program was designed to provide an income without having to enter the job market. It successfully destroyed the will to achieve. Lastly, it destroyed the family by imposing a rule that a non-working male (father) could not reside in a house receiving a Welfare check.

The introduction of drugs in black society was designed to kill the spirit, drive, and motivation.

The de-education of blacks was achieved through the integration of schools in non-integrated neighborhoods. Whites moved to reestablish segregated schools that were sufficiently funded school systems in segregated neighborhoods with strong tax bases, leaving black schools in poor neighborhoods with low, insufficient tax bases. Thus, began the creation of a really bad education for black kids with the intent of killing their ability to be competitive in the economic market place. African Americans are now in the process of rebuilding the foundation of any society, the family unit.

Reestablishing Fatherhood

In nineteen sixty only nine percent of all children lived in single- parent homes. Presently in the United States, almost one third of children are born to single mothers. A larger number of children will see their parents divorced before their eighteenth birthday. Two third of black kids are born out of wedlock. Over half of American children will spend all or part of their childhood without their father in the home.

Robert Rector of the Heritage Foundation cited that the collapse of marriage is the principal cause of child poverty and *other social problems. Half of the children are living without the support and attention of their fathers, and have never been in their father's home, or those over the age of four never saw their fathers at least once a week. Those statistics must change.*

Though the effort should be applauded, It is too much to expect a single mother to raise a boy to become a man. In most societies it is the responsibility of the elder men to assist in the development of boys into men. It now must be the responsibility of the elder or mature African American males to prepare the young men.

The time is now for the black college fraternities and sororities to share in the mentoring and surrogate fathering of young fatherless black kids. It is not too much to ask fraternities and sororities to take on the responsibility for mentoring those fatherless kids by sponsoring a monthly breakfast to just talk.

New elders it is time to step up. It's your turn. It takes a village… There should be a similar expectation of the sororities. Reach back, take a struggling little girl by the hand, and show her the way.

Success would only require an honest commitment, because contrary to popular belief, black kids have very high self-esteem.

Although it is a common myth that black youth are likely to have low self-esteem, studies in the last few decades have shown them to feel just as good, if not better, about themselves and as self-confident, in general, as white youth; the only thing that they need are direction and guidance. They need someone to teach them life skills. Someone to show them the way. Step up Greek sisters and brothers.

Faith Based Education

Historically, the church played a pivotal role in black society. It provided spiritual sustenance, faith education, and a sense of safety in the lord. It baptized the newborn, and buried the departed. In our new world the church must expand its role to provide focused survival skills.

The Wednesday bible study classes, in addition to faith based training, it should include classes in wealth building. Why introduce wealth building in faith building classes? Because there is no better opportunity to reach that group that would most benefit for the education. Bible study classes are usually attended by people that gave up that time to learn. They are, in some cases, those who would benefit from understanding how the credit systems work. They need to understand the danger of Pay Day Loans, or car loans. They are the victims of these predatory practices because of a lack of understanding. Classes would prevent them from being victimized.

In addition to teaching people how not to become victims, they need to understand how to develop wealth, how to prepare to become home owners. When they came to the church to learn how to build their faith, they leave with a faith in their ability to survive financially. The are a willing , captive audience.

8

Media Matter

PERCEPTIONS ARE FORMED BY *what you see and hear. The perceptions of African Americans are shaped by the media locally, nationally, and internationally. Occasionally, ratings are the driving force in what is aired; therefore the media portrays African Americans as ignorant, lazy, irresponsible, welfare grubbing, drug infected, and dangerous. In most instances we are robbing, selling drugs, or raping. It is not unusual for foreign visitors to feel threatened in the presence of black people.*

Black staffs in hotels are constantly reminded by foreign guest that they are uncomfortable in their presence because of how they are portrayed in the media. It is not unusual for a guest at hotels to call for service at night, yet they refused to open the door if they see a black staff person. They usually request that you return in the morning when they feel safer.

Most media representation of black kids is that they are slow learners, discipline problems, and mostly products of single parent, struggling homes. The really sad thing is that the more kids see this image of them the more they tend to believe it.

Negative propaganda is insidious, in most news pieces that are about unemployment, the featured character is usually black. If the issue is positive and uplifting, the featured character is white. In news articles about drug abuse, if the outcome is negative, the character is always black. Take the same story featuring a white character, the person is in successful rehab, and now enrolled at Harvard.

When this type of propaganda is constantly shown, it is only reasonable to conclude that, blacks always fail, and whites will always succeed.

The media cannot be held totally responsible; we have those among us who will not pass up any opportunity to be, "master's house niggah." They will sell out their culture and themselves just to be noticed. Turn on the camera and lights, and some black folk will act like newly freed slaves. They will denigrate themselves and their race. This only perpetuates the image of no dingy or self respect. Professional athletes are sometimes the worse offenders. However, I am always proud when I watch a LeBron James, Cleveland Cavaliers. Every interview is thoughtful, articulate, and informative. He is more representative of the new athlete.

About three or four years ago, radio talk show host, Don Imus took the liberty of referring to a mostly black women's college basketball team as a bunch of "NAPPU HEADED HO'S". Imus's reputation was as a loose tongue, say anything morning radio host, with millions of loyal fans. His list of sponsors was impressive. His earnings were in the millions of dollars. His friends were among the most powerful in the business sector, and government. Yet when he made that statement on that morning, his sponsor support immediately dried up. What followed only served to validate my long held position that, America is about the almighty dollar, and it will not allow anyone or anything to influence that.

This incident should have served as a awakening for black folk, because what followed was enlightening. From this insult came corporate America's response to the threat to their almighty dollar.

Don Imus had insulted a population that had a GDP value of almost a TRILLION DOLLARS. A large part is used to purchase products that sponsor the Don Imus Show. Corporate America had to make a decision about what African American's response would be about the insult, and how they would feel about those who would sponsor it. Black folk could abandon their products. ONE TRILLION DOLLARS in buying power was about to abandon their brands. Corporate America made a swift and decisive decision, DROP IMUS NOW.

African Americans should have come away from that experience with an understanding that ONR TRILLION DOLLARS in spending power is louder than ten Million Man Marches. Your value, your dignity is in the volume of your money. Your protest should no longer be protest marches; it should be the threat of withholding your money. Your power is your money. African Americans should understand that; if they were a separate country, it would be the tenth riches country in the world. We don't have to accept commercial abuse anymore.

The Imus story was not to relate an insult in the media. The real purpose of the Imus story was to encourage black to never allow themselves to be victims again. When the media chose to take liberties with our dignity, don't complain to the media, complain to the sponsors. With ONE TRILLION in your wallet you should never feel like a victim again.

From this day forward, we should warn the media that you can not portray black Americans in that insulting way again.

9

Summary

APRIL, 1968 THE DEATH of Dr. Martin Luther King started
black folk in America on a journey to find the Promise Land.
After 300 years of slavery and all the misery, indignation,
and deprivation that supported slavery, we embarked on
that forty year journey. Some understood that there would
be long hard days ahead. They understood that there were
behaviors, mental programming, and deficient educational
preparation that would have to be eliminated before we
entered the Promise Land. And so we wandered...

During that time; we fought with the idol (drugs)
worshipers; the propagandists (media); and the power
structure (money and politics) to prepare to begin building

a productive society once we entered. Very few people realized that the basic infrastructure was in place to build a society of which to be proud.

The first notable change is the emergence of the new Elders (new young leadership) to take on the responsibility for developing the next generations.

Over the past forty years, contrary to media propaganda, a clear understanding of the importance of education has increased the focus on developing alternative school systems. Now educational options like charter schools, voucher programs, military academies, and gender based alternatives are being developed.

Post high school career paths are part of the new curriculum, for example; vocational educational skills development; IT and other technical programs are seriously under consideration; and finally, school to career union apprentice programs are slowly being structured.

Strong emphasis will always drive Advance Placement preparation. Post high school education is always the desired path. Some will not be able to exercise that option upon graduation, so the school to work option should be available.

Historically Black Colleges and Universities (HBCU) s are a under utilized national treasure for black kids. The problem is that in some instances they sometimes lack proper management and necessary funding to competitively prepare black students for the market place.

This can be fixed. This must be fixed to provide black students a black educational option- their option for an education in a nurturing environment that is black centric. But first, these schools must be developed as a resource. Our resource....

Wealth building is the next most important element in the development of a proud, strong black segment of this American society. We have the wealth, it's just not focused. I used the term Bling-Bling broke to explain the value that we some times placed on black wealth. *I have since come to realize that the new elders are becoming major player in this country. They are starting to buy shares in the wealth producers*

JZ (Hip Hop mogul) for example, own a share in a NBA team. **Tyler Perry owns a movie studio, and Oprah owns everything. The new elders have stared to become sophisticated in the amassing and managing wealth. They now have the dignity that that bring. They understand the value of their money. It time for the rest of black society to understand the power of money. It time to understand that wealth brings dignity.**

Lastly, political power, the vote in America is political power. In 2008 African Americans elected a president, a black president. Such was unimaginable any other time in history. Yet by unity of effort we saw our dreams- no Martin Luther King's dream realized. It took unity of purpose and a dream. Therefore we must never become complacent- whites will take back your dingy, your wealth, and your dream.

Tell Martin that we fulfilled his dream- we got to the promised land. Now we must begin to build that shining city on the hill, the city that we can all be proud of. Our city.

Foot Notes

Photograph of J. Seward Johnson, Jr.'s "The Awakening" located Hains Point, Washington D.C. Photographer

Introduction

Speech by Martin Luther King in Memphis, Tenn. April 3, 1998

Chapter 1

1. Excerpts from Ordinary Children, Extraordinary Teachers and Marva Collins' Way.
2. Ibid
3. Ibid
4. Ibid

Paul Tough January/February 2009 Issue

5. What Ever it Takes
6. Ibid
7. Ibid
8. Kathy Piechura-Couture, Stetson University
9. Ibid
10. Ibid
11. Ibid
12. Ibid
13. Ibid
14. Ibid

15. Ibd
16. Ibid
17. Ibid
18. Ibid
19. Ibid
20. Ibid
21. Ten-hut! Are public military high schools good for teens? Nov 12, 2007
    COPYRIGHT 2007 Weekly Reader Corp.
22. Ibid
23. Ibid
24. Ibid
25. Ibid
26. Ibid
27. Ibid
28. Ibid
29. Ibid
30. Ibid
31. Ibid
32. Ibid
33. California Department of Education

After School Learning and Safe Neighborhoods Partnerships Program released in 2002

34. Ibid
35. Ibid
36. Ibid
37. Ibid
38. Ibid
39. Ibid
40. Ibid
41. Ibid
42. Ibid
43. Ibid
44. Ibid

The Bill & Melinda Gates Foundation

2   Ibid.

3   Carey, Kevin, "Choosing to Improve: Voices from Colleges and Universities with Better Graduation Rates," Washington, DC: Achieve, 2005. No source cited.

4   Peter D. Hart Research Associates, "Rising to the Challenge: Are High School Graduates Prepared for College and Work," Washington, DC: Achieve, 2005.

5   American Diploma Project, "Ready Or Not: Creating a High School Diploma That Works," Washington, DC: Achieve, Inc, 2004.

6   Johnson J. and Duffet, A., "Where We Are Now: 12 Things You Need to Know About Public Opinion and Public Schools," NY: Public Agenda, 2002. Reality Check.

7   Carnevale, Anthony and Desrochers, Donna, "Standards for What? The Economic Roots of K-16 Reform," Washington, DC: Educational Testing Service, 2004.

8   Sum, Andrew; Khatiwada, Ishwar; Pond, Nathan; and Trub'skyy, Mykhaylo, "Left Behind in the Labor Market: Labor Market Problems of the Nation's Out-of-School, Young Adult Populations," prepared for the Alternative Schools Network, Boston: Center for Labor Market Studies, Northeastern University, 2002.

9   National Center for Education Statistics, "Remedial Education at Degree-Granting Postsecondary Institutions in Fall 2000," Washington, DC: U.S. Department of Education, 2003.

10 Carnevale and Desrochers, 2004.

11 Baum, Sandy and Payea, Kathleen, "Education Pays: The Benefits of Higher Education for Individuals and Society," NJ: College Board, 2004.

3. Explaining why African-American boys lag in school -- and deciding what to do about it
Tuesday, July 29, 2003
By Larry E. Davis

4. What is a historically black college/university (HBCU)?
8/27/2008 By Liz Funk Provided by: Next Step Magazine

Chapter 2

1. *School-to-Career*

A QUICK GUIDE for Organized Labor

2. 25 Highest-Paying Jobs for High School Grads HR.BLR.com's Salary Center

Chapter 3

1. List of Wealthiest African-Americans

From Wikipedia, the free encyclopedia Retrieved from _http://_
_en.wikipedia.org/wiki/List_of_Wealthiest_African-Americans_"

2. Cathy Mickens of Neighborhood Housing Services in Jamaica, Queens.
3. Ibid
4. Boston College Center on Wealth and Philanthropy (CWP) projects(April 18, 2005
5. Ibid
6. Warmed-over Myths of Black Wealth
7. Ibid
8. Newsflash from CNBC's NEWBOs: If you're black and can't rap or play ball, forget about making it in America.
   By Alfred Edmond, Jr. – February 27, 2009

9. Ibid
10. Ibid

Chapter 4

1. Do Democrats need the black vote?
   By Robert Schlesinger
   April 4, 2008...12:02 pm
2. Ibid

Chapter 5

1. **Black Fraternities Thrive, Often on Adversity**
   By ISABEL WILKERSON
   Published: Monday, October 2, 1989
2. *The Connecticut Coalition for Achievement NOW*

Mr. James C. Rollins is a native of Washington D.C. He currently resides in Fort Washington, Maryland. Mr. Rollins served in the United States Air Force from 1961-1965. He later attended Antioch University where he pursued a Bachelor of Science in Business Administration. He retired from the District of Columbia Government in 1995.

Mr. Rollins, author of the controversial book "The Curse of Willie Lynch: How social engineering in the year 1712 continues to affect African Americans today," is an impassioned person who says he seeks change within the African American community. Mr. Rollins decision to write the book rests on an incident involving his youngest daughter who was enrolled in a competitive Chicago medical school. Recently that same daughter graduated with honors. She is now Dr. Rollins.

Rollins' book, published in 2006 by Trafford Publishing, tried to identify the sources for the lack of self confidence African American children face in society.

He writes of his fellow African-Americans, "We are the only ethnic group that has come to depend on someone to lead us, to articulate our dreams, and negotiate ... for our rights." After the conversation with his youngest daughter, Rollins knew he had a moral obligation to put his thoughts to paper. In a three-month fury of research and writing, Rollins completed what he considers one of the most meaningful works of his life. Since then, Rollins has developed a sizeable following with his easy, down-to-earth writing style and potent beliefs.

Mr. Rollins, through numerous book singings and public speaking endeavors, passionately desires to empower African American youth with the optimistic reality of their potential. He maintains that, "If you don't teach our kids that they have worth and value, if you teach them that what they see on BET is who they are, then we can't expect anything more than that. ... But I want them to know that we don't need to beg for a seat of the table, that we have a power to control what happens in our community and in our lives."